P9-DCE-861

To Janet & George

with thanks

Just Married

by Stan Galloway

[signed] Stan Galloway

unbound CONTENT

Englewood, NJ

ISBN 978-1-936373-36-9
© 2013 Stan Galloway. All rights reserved. No part of this publication may be reproduced or transmitted in any form or by any means, electronic or mechanical, without permission in writing from the publisher. Requests for permission to make copies of any part of this work should be e-mailed to info@unboundcontent.com.
Published in the United States by Unbound Content, LLC, Englewood, NJ.
Cover art: Nude Model in the Studio ©2012, by Charles Scogins
Author photo: ©2013, by Cara Zimmerman Walton

Just Married

First edition 2013

For Denise Levertov (1923-1997),
who first made poetry come alive for me

Table of Contents

The Rehearsal..11

Wedding Dress..12

The Wedding Scripture...13

At the Reception 14

Just Married..15

20 July...16

Touching Palms...17

Honolulu Elevator 19

Unpacking the Suitcase 20

The Piano Promise...21

Tan Lines..22

Walking on the Beach 23

Next-to-Last Night 24

Eating Ice Cream at Midnight..25

First Day at Work After the Honeymoon 26

How We Kiss..27

The Art of Introduction...28

Puddle Jumping...29

My Clothes 30

Morning Coffee...31

Piggyback...32

Carnival...33

Feeding Ducks..34

Your Shoes...35

The Tourniquet..36

Spirit Touch..37

Across the Table..38

Perfect Seven..39

Putting Away Laundry 40

Ironing...41

Toenails...42

Writing and Reading 43

The Thing We Shared..44

Waking...46

Changing Oil...48

Museum Visit 50

Eating Cereal..52

Counterplay..53

Company Picnic 54

Morning Glory 55

Necklace...56

Hands...57

Post-Fireworks...58

Sunburn...59

Carwash...60

Bee Sting..61

Folding Laundry While You Are Away..............................62

Soft Scent...63

Hole Nine...64

I Took Three Books 65

Balcony Flower 66

Buying Sanitary Napkins...67

I Smell Onions 68

Sick Day..69

Watching You Sleep...70

Making Progress..71

Visit 72

Old Photograph...73

Your Mother's Scar 74

The Stars Last Night...75

Fretting..76

Tuesday Morning Thanks...77

Weekend 78

Reverie 82

Morning Hair...83

Hair Drying 84

Three-Month Anniversary 86

Delight 87

Making Love the Hundredth Time 88

Missing You 89

Hat 90

Tire-Changing 91

Celebrate 92

Next Best 93

Scraping the Windshield 94

Watching You Read in Bed 95

Apology 96

Shopping 97

Watching Football 98

Pie Making 99

Seeing Straight 100

Giving Space 101

Milk Jug 102

Storm Thoughts 103

Car Show 104

Weighing In 105

Some Kinds of Love 106

Nursing the Kitten 107

The Ring 108

Long Lunch 109

Remembering Waikiki 110

Headache 111

Cleaning the Tub 112

Sable Dress 113

Rust 114

Makeup 115

Mapping Spilled Milk 116

Cooking Pasta 117

Just Married 2 118

Winter Weather 119

About the Author 121

Publication Credits 123

The Rehearsal

Who are all these crazy women
trying to make *our* wedding
be the one they never had?
Relatives and mother's friends,
I understand,
but why the yelling and the arguing?
And the minister who thinks
his night job is comedian—
where did he come from?
I've seen better circuses.
And when you say tonight
is so the jitters
all get worked out,
I do remember
I am not the only one
who matters here—
but still, I wonder,
is it too late to elope?

Wedding Dress

At last,
I see you in the dress
that marks the day
I thought would never come.

You radiate
like some aurora from the north,
condoning just this once
a private form.

I like
the white rice-lace layered look
with silk and saffron accents
at the cuffs and hem,
the puzzling opacity
beneath an airy openness
that weds
disclosure with complexity.

It fits you well,
the way I hope
to fit you ever after.

The Wedding Scripture

Does the Bible really say
        love does not boast?
I want to boast that I found you—
        I'll raise a toast.

And envy surely has a place
        when good is sought.
I envy every man you've kissed
        for what he's got.

Love does not seek to get its way
        but yields the claim.
I yield to you on anything
        except my name.

No grudges—really?—how's that done?
        I've got no clue,
but I'm content to learn that skill—
        I'll learn with you.

At the Reception

Hugging, hugged, and pawed by many other friendly hands than yours,
while you stand by and hug the same unnumbered friends and family,
when now the only hands I want on me are yours, and mine on you;
kissing, both of us, politely, fifty closest relatives,
when kissing should be simply my lips/your lips all alone together;
eating cake not moist enough, the heavy icing overdried,
in contrast to the moist reception, natural glaze, you hold for me;
considering obligatory nuts and mints together taunting,
auguring the tastes of me and you that we anticipate;
and drinking frothy, fruity punch, a fragrant pledge deprived of truth,
when nothing else can satisfy my thirst but you, and you alone;
intolerably waiting, passing time required by tradition,
plastic smiles covering our bloods' unspoken scream and plea
to lie beside each other in the bedrest promised us at last.

Just Married

The sanctioned moment has arrived
And we may exit tactfully.

The cake is portioned out, some punch
Still cupped, the nuts and mints askew.

Your hand in mine, we boldly move
Toward the exit, leading all.

The sweeping, scrubbing up the spills
Will fall to others, thankfully.

The limo marks our great escape
Amid the birdshot-turned-confetti.

Cheers and waves from relatives
Hide winks from bridal party friends.

"Just Married" reads the trailing kite
Someone has rigged to hover aft.

But promptly at the second light
It breaks its tether—just like us.

20 July

Decades back, this day,
a man stepped on the moon,
and planted deep a flag for every human,
culmination of a billion dreams
and source of pride around the world.

Today I held your hand
and looked into your eyes—
you kissed me and
invited me to come to bed with you,
my private dream come true
my pride,
the milestone
I give my life to claim.

Touching Palms

Everything is new
foreign and familiar:

The water unreal blue
stretches beneath us
rising closer
as the runway races, seizing us
just out of water's reach.

A Filipino woman checks our bag tags,
and I wheel the cart to curbside,
hail a cab,
and feel the journey's end beginning.

The golden-edged green fingers of the trees
reach out to us in greeting—
feathers, free and independent,
like the ones we're testing even now
on this, ironically, our maiden flight.

The air is heavy
with anticipation and relief,
every turn a first,
a deja vu,
a fantasy in flesh
that makes me pinch myself,
and you.

And in the room at last,
I take your cheeks between my fingers
and see again the woman of my dreams.
We kiss and walk out to the balcony,
shaded by the trees,
look across the beach to happy water,
comfortable,
touching palms.

Honolulu Elevator

Alone together,
going up too fast,
you looked into my eyes
and leaned toward me.

Our lips met
at the center of the universe,
the walls blurring
to indistinction,
while a nova
birthed a galaxy
inside me.

Unpacking the Suitcase

I don't remember my eyes opening—
but suddenly you filled my vision, sorting
through the suitcase, three feet from me, naked
just from bed, a red crease on your back where
you had lain on something folded over
or perhaps my arm that tingled at
that moment. You were choosing clothing for
the day, a tank top but no bra, a thong,
and running shorts, an easy choice to walk
along the beach first thing. But there were many
other things you'd packed, things unexpected—
books, for instance, and a movie with a
title not quite legible, a letter
that appeared quite old. Your skin I knew
to some degree but it was then I knew
I'd never fully know what you were carrying,
except as you revealed it one thing at a time.

The Piano Promise

The piano in the hotel meeting room
caught your whim and
you veered to it
on our way out to the beach.

You sat and tapped
a halting Chopsticks
then invited me to join.

I said I'd never learned,
and so we started out again,
while you said you
would show me that
and several other things you've learned
before the week is ended.

Tan Lines

Your tan lines say "I love you" to me.

After lying out, the marks of bold
whiteness on those special areas
delineate the sight that other
beachside watchers could not see, but in
the hotel bathroom everything is
bared as you prepare for dinner out.
Geometric shapes mix and meld in
private ways, accentuate the fine
body marks that are distinctly yours.
That you are unashamed to see me
see you, invite inspection by your
look, says I am a man apart from
every other in your favor.

Walking on the Beach

Walking on the beach
with you by Diamond Head,
beneath a moon as large
as anything, I find
my tongue unable to
express the happiness
I feel. Your hand in mine
won't settle, pulsing, squeezing,
telling me that what
our tongues can't say our bodies
know. We stop and let
tied tongues touch instead.

Next-to-Last Night

I never knew my nipples would respond like yours
until you demonstrated in the honeymoon
hotel room. You had gotten me a pair of silk
pajamas and were patient since it wasn't 'til
the next-to-last night that I even put them on.
You took your thumbnail and your fingers and began
to slowly rake across the fabric, wide across
my chest at first, an odd massage or phantom rabbit
trail that hopped the tinder point repeatedly,
the trail contracting like my skin as you honed in
and made the male anomaly begin to stand,
to reach for more, to feel the synthesis of silk
and sexual arousal, softly coaxed by firm
material attention, supple, strangely soft,
aggressively applied. While we did other things
that night, the great awakening was that
the ways that we are one, mysterious, had one more link—
the sympathy my body had innately tuned with yours.

Eating Ice Cream at Midnight

We should be sleeping but this honeymoon's
last   night's   darkness must not fall.
We keep the lights   bright. We want to tease
and squeeze the final pleasant moment to
extreme, so share a monstrous Baskin-Robbins,
licking, each in turn, to keep   time's
drippings in control,   giggling, giddy,
closed to morning's flight to home and work
and normalcy.   One   small vanilla
drip escapes us, staining white the swimsuit
top you wear in pseudo-modesty.
I hold the cone while your   deft   fingers
slip the knots. I watch you rinse the fabric
in the sink just long enough to keep
the stain from taking. With   wet   hands,
you return with your   two   scoops,
defined by this   week's   tan   lines,
French vanilla, cherry-topped, inviting
my   cold   tongue to prod the fruit
upright. We   sit   close without the
pretense of restraint and find inherent
instability—unable to
prohibit, we pursue. This night, the ice
cream will not last—we strain to swallow it
before it melts away.

First Day at Work After the Honeymoon

Last year's models clog the lot—
Too many—something must be done
To make what's old seem something hot,
What's ordinary now seem fun.

Why bother when the fun still calls—
We'll both be home at half past six—
And what's behind the bedroom walls
Is hot with no pretended fix.

But selling's how I pay the bills—
Responsibility's a must—
A job well done precedes the thrills
Of evening hours' love and lust.

How We Kiss

When you kiss me
and your eyelids flutter
showing slips of white,
I know your pleasure
is embodied somewhere
deep inside,
contracted to the seed
of your desire.

Every quiver,
        shift,
               and arc
is made to draw that point
to its most concentrated form.

I know because I watch your eyes
(and feel your lips) with mine,
resisting any risk
of losing sight of you,
a woman of reality
not dreams.

So every kiss,
an act of reason
and deliberate commission,
will be given with
wide-open eyes.

Stan Galloway

The Art of Introduction
(*In the Peristyle*, John William Waterhouse, 1874)

While waiting at the office for my boss,
I couldn't help but notice a display
of prints by Waterhouse. A few of them
I'd seen before—the Lady of Shallott,
the mermaid, and Ophelia—but the one
that caught my eye was of a young girl with
a woven basket, feeding pigeons. She was
stopped mid-motion, height mature but face
still adolescent, fit and innocent,
her white chemise displaying subtle motion.
Her simplicity reminded me
of you, and of the day beside the tennis
courts when I first saw you in your tennis
whites. Some swifts had gathered on the fence,
the way the doves atop the colonnade
look down into the court where Waterhouse's
unnamed girl dispenses seed to half
a dozen brave and hungry souls. I was
the white one to her right, I think, just watching,
asking if I could be brave enough
to catch your gaze, or errant ball. Your eyes
were tracking boys off to your left—the way
this bird-enamored girl is—watchers and
participants appreciating form,
the way your arm swung wide, the grace embodied
in a natural gesture: much like tossing
seed to see which ones would venture nearer.
Love and *match* were on my mind from that day
on, but it took several weeks before
I turned your head and I sent every other
bird retreating to the frieze to watch.

Puddle Jumping

After rain had left
a hundred puddles in the street,
you and I went walking
hand in hand
to watch the sunset.

At first we skirted,
        dodged,
           and hopped across each tiny lake,
  until you caught one with your heel,
splashing
         random
       spray across my knee
and up your calf and thigh.

Your laugh infected me and
together our feet aimed not over
         but bull's-eye
       in the next one,
      and the next ...

Long past the dusk
we walked home under streetlights,
dripping from the navel down,
and I was eight years old again.

And you beside me, I wonder,
How old were you?

My Clothes

I like it when you wear my clothes,
because it says you want reminders
of me on you, ones that say,
"You're special," or "I like your different
size and style." And I like the
looseness that allows me peeks of
you beneath in general household
movements. Most of all I like
to think you wear my shirt or running
shorts so that when next I wear them our two
skins can touch throughout the day by proxy.

Morning Coffee

"There is no morning
Till this cup's empty"—
I had read the cup a hundred times
but I never understood it
before the morning that I saw you
standing naked in the kitchen
staring where the rising sun
lit the dust above the counter.
Your phone was tweedling for attention
and the odor of forgotten bacon
was threatening to trip the smoke alarm,
but you stood resolute, a lighthouse
oblivious to any storm,
sipping life
from monochrome
to color.

Piggyback

Carrying you piggyback,
holding tight your thighs against my sides,
your hands encircling my neck
and chin bobbing just above my hair,
your hair playing tag
with my ears and cheeks.
your body leaned against me,
gently rocking (kiss, release)
with every step—

When will we grow too old for simple childlike embracing,
                too old to celebrate the day entwined together,
                too old to carry one another?

That day will never come,
I vow,
though hugging
        holding
        carrying
won't always look like this.

Carnival

Why anyone would want
(or make) a three-foot stuffed
banana, I don't know,
but you said, "Win that for me,"
and I couldn't dis-
appoint—twenty-seven
tries it took, nine dollars
by the foot, but it was
worth the smile that you
wore for me, and it,
for hours even when
the carnival had closed its
gates and we were snuggled
into bed, all three.

Feeding Ducks

I dare not laugh,
but when I watch you throwing stale bread
to the mallards at the park,
it's obvious you didn't play much baseball as a kid—
your pitches wobble
like those ducklings trying out their wings
and plop like windfall
helter-skelter.
But the mallards never seem to care
because they come to every scrap you throw,
the way that I do
every time that you extend your hand.

Your Shoes

Black patent leather
Holding toes and tender arch
Until I rub them

The Tourniquet

We'd hiked much farther than intended when it
happened. Slippery trail-edge rocks sent both
of us into the creek, three inches deep.
It wasn't 'til I tried to stand that pain
informed me it had been less innocent
that we had thought. A gash along my shin
was bleeding badly, so I rinsed it, hoping
it would stop, and you applied some pressure
at the edges, trying to restrict
the flow, to help coagulation. Funny
now, I can't remember what we said,
but after several minutes I suggested
you tear off a portion of my shirt
and make a bandage. But instead you slipped
your own shirt off, unhooked your bra, and tightly
wound it round and round until you got it
hooked again, a makeshift tourniquet,
the silliest and prettiest I'd ever
seen. The trail was long returning, but I
didn't mind, your arm around my back,
me squeezed inside your bra, us walking slowly,
stopping often, getting frequent stares
from other passersby. The ER doctor
complimented your resourceful work
and seven stitches later he was done.
He'd never seen a tourniquet like that
before. It represented one more proof
of thousands of your daily love for me.

Spirit Touch

In your sleep
you reached out to me,
just a motion,
loose and free,
and I felt a tug within me,
spirit reaching out to spirit,
speaking underneath unconscious breathing,
quiet,
      trusting,
            calm contentment.
So I place
my hand over yours
and let our spirits
touch as well.

Across the Table

There's something about
watching you eat,
not erotic per se,
but sensual,
the way your tongue
guides each bite in,
delicately with the tip
to just the place
where teeth will grip it
and the lips surround it,
sealing it.
And with each up-and-down
the jaw makes,
the skin of your cheeks
undulates like clouds in motion
and your throat
in confidence and gentleness
contracts with each small swallow
as you savor the taste
on your tongue
of each new food.
The natural roundness
of your lips in motion
gives me thought for food.

Perfect Seven

Raoul and Lola taught me more than "Crazy Sevens" when they
visited last night. The cards were fun and fairly simple,
and the *cochinillo* sweetly seasoned, but the thing that
I learned most was how to honor *mi muher* in little
ways. *Siete Loco* was the framework for the lesson,
sure, but when the cards are stacked away and *Martes* is
forgotten, three things stick: the *deferencia* that any
loving man should make, like offering the seat with better
light and pouring *vino* only to her limit, noting
not the thing she says she wants but offering the thing
she needs; and then there is *la boca*, as Raoul was fond of saying,
that discerns the moment to be *abierto o*
cerrada, closing every time the woman starts to speak,
as if her words were oracles from heaven; finally,
I saw in them *comunicacion* between their eyes
that Lola made, a simple look that signaled it was time
to go, a telepathic word, if I believed such things
could be—I want that intimate connection so that when
you look at me, I understand exactly what you mean.
If being Mexican is what it takes, I'll eat more pork
and play more cards and even get my Spanish primer out,
so one day you can have the same awareness, perfect "seven"
every time, and I can be the lover you deserve.

Putting Away Laundry

You left the laundry stacked
beside the heart-shaped pillow that I gave you
on the sofa.

You will put it all away
when you return from shopping—
if I leave it.

But the heart I gave you
tells me I should finish for you.
One trip to the kitchen
with the dish towels.
One trip to the bathroom
with the wash cloths.
Two trips to the bedroom
where your underwear and socks
are slipped into your top drawer,
followed next by mine.

I go back to the sofa,
listening for what my heart
will tell me next.

Ironing

Even the common is charged with excitement when
you, unselfconsciously, iron your shirt in the
morning. Your hair is just dried and your panties cling
deftly around ample buttocks that flex when you
push for the collar end. I'm still in bed thinking
Saturday never should end—but it must—so I
promise myself when you finish I'll get up and
shower, but watching you smooth out the fabric to
match the smooth skin it will cover enthralls me. I
watch as your right arm moves rhythmically forward and
back, with your breasts, small and high, keeping time to the
motion. Each sleeve, every seam, and the placket get
focused attention, the way that you focused on
me when we cuddled and kissed just the evening
before when we practiced a similar rhythm
together. Now shifting the cloth you so carefully
poke at the pocket edge, snatch up the shirt with a
satisfied flourish that matches my galloping
heart, and return to the bathroom. I'll follow you.

Toenails

When I asked if I could paint your toenails,
you responded with a look of shock,
as if I'd asked to pinch your nose or something,
even though you wore a simple towel-turban,
nothing else, and I no towel at all.
You smiled after that,
extended to my lap your foot
and handed me the bottle you had opened.

Though my first time doing this
required coaching from you,
you were patient and encouraged me.

Then later,
after we had dressed for dinner,
I had a silly grin
whenever you stepped out
and showed those toes,
reminding me
that I had been with you
the way no other man has been.

Writing and Reading

Staying up long with my work's obligations, I'm
late with reports for the manager's office and
fearing I'm spurning my wife's expectations. While
filling out forms on my lap for my quota, I
      glance at you and wish I were your book, but
keeping my job is important, essential to
      fund the dinners, gifts, and flowers given
from all the sales of the automobiles which in
      form are nothing like your smooth, sleek markings.
Paperwork, legal forms, deaden my senses,
      revived by sight of you now propped with book—
sufficiently different from anything I must read—
      warming thought, and skin exposed from waist up,
topless like best-selling sports cars on Market Street,
      calls me, subtle movement of your breathing
rippling like flags on September's new models, yet
      nearly still, still whitened from our first week,
      breasts that read along with eyes, relaxed,
      alert to heroine's delightful plot twists
      held in place by tented legs in covers.

The Thing We Shared

You carried away the
bag of leftovers
from the restaurant,
a double helping of the
rice we didn't touch and
some spicy shrimp asparagus.

We walked under
misted streetlights
on wet sidewalks,
you holding that bag
and my hand
as we passed
Zales and Macy's
even Morgan's Books
without our steps
or your head turning,
and we talked of weather,
and the news,
and Canada geese.
You said you liked the
geese because they mate
for life, and the
smile you gave me then
all but called me gander.

Just Married

When we reached home
you put the bag in the
refrigerator and led me
on a Hansel-Gretel trail
of socks and bra
up to the loft. You said
you cherish everything
we have together.

Near midnight you descended,
opened up the bag
to taste again
the thing we shared.

Waking

Waking to the pleasure
of your presence,
I feel your warmth
before anything else,
hear you gently breathing.
The sleepy sunlight cottoning my eyelids
tells me morning is approaching
and that soon the clock will sound
to send me to my day.

But I will not climb out of bed until the sound,
treasuring
these unexpected moments.
I see you lying
beside me,
the rumpled sheet tangled
at your hip.
You are where I saw you last,
touched you last,
and smelled you,
sweet and sweat,
and tasted salt.

From where my head lies,
I see one nipple,
soft in night's flaccidity,
a low-angle,
soft-focus glamour shot
for my single viewing.

Just Married

Your breast rises slowly and
recedes with your breathing,
the sunlight dancing
on the gentle body hairs
that go unnoticed
except when everything else
rests
and the sunrise angel
glazes your skin.

I can't resist extending
one finger
to dimple its softness,
and marvel
at its conciliating presence.
Then I move my mouth
to your neck and cheek,
kissing,
rubbing lightly,
till the flutter of your eye
prompts me to withdraw
and watch
one bold nipple,
newly roused,
and see you
waking to the presence
of your pleasure.

Changing Oil

Sloppy,
     wet,
       and dark,
          the oil gurgles,
              spatters to the drain pan,
while I thread the filter into place.
                 I'm covered by the unjacked pickup,
except where my two legs
        protrude
        between the passenger-side tires.
                Then I hear,
"How long till you're done?"
        Before I can respond,
            I feel your tennis shoe
                  rest
gently
    on my groin
      and rock a message left unsaid.
           I slide myself enough to get
               a view.
One eye
    sees the truck frame,
        one eye
          follows from the ankle
             up
              the smooth

Just Married

tanned leg
        to where
                my running shorts hang poofy on you,
                                 loose in this
                                         inverted
view,
    revealing that
              dark patch and
                      gentle line
                            so known and treasured
                                  in that other context.
"I've got to plug it, fill it up."
                   "How long?"
                          With one hand working blindly,
frantically, I say,
        "A few more minutes,
                      then
                    I'll come
                        with you
                            inside."

Museum Visit

I had no desire to attend
the drab reception at the old museum.
But I went because it seemed a better
choice than sitting home alone.
I'm grateful for the trip you gave me,
one enchanted evening unexpected.

For a moment it was like we'd hopped
into a Mary Poppins sidewalk drawing.
We pretended Roman pillars
were the trees of Arden forest,
talking back to age-old portraits—
rails and velvet bumpers were
the boundaries of our playground.
You boathooked my arm
and promenaded on the boardwalk,
then we waltzed around a statue of Demeter,
nude above the waist—
you wagged your shoulders at me
like a wannabe of Marilyn Monroe,
and when you jumped the bench
beside the fountain I reached out
and tapped your flying buttress.
Underneath a Roman frieze,
you kissed me,
pointing to a viny mass
misread as mistletoe.

Just Married

Then all too soon,
we stood with twenty other patrons,
dreary as a foggy street,
and you leaned on my arm
and whispered there was
plenty other art and architecture
to explore when we got home.

Eating Cereal

New! Improved! Bigger! Better!
Compare to other leading brands.
Daily intake x-percent—
insufficient overall
without a supplement or two.

Seeing you across the box top flap,
I realize that eating cereal
is not like being married.
I'm not looking for someone new.
Improvement is a possibility, but
I don't need you bigger,
and better is a relative concern.
I don't need to make comparisons
to know I'm satisfied with what we have.
I don't need more than you each day,
no supplement would ever strengthen me
beyond what we together can produce.

Counterplay

Humming some old eighties tune
you say your father sang to you
when you were young,
you wipe the counter down,
corral some crumbs into the trash,
and swish the sink
as if the daily cleaning
were a joy.

I know it's not,
but somehow when the duty
has a tune,
the drudgery diffuses,
and I realize
if I would join you,
we could clean
in half the time
in stereo.

Company Picnic

The picnic for the dealership
was fun, I thought, despite the brick
that scraped my shin when Evan's son
collapsed the fire pit. The crepes
were great, as were the bratwursts slapped
on at the end. I really ate
more than I should have. You, the "fat one"
in your dreams, ate little, dancing
here and there, your nametag scrawled
a bit illegible, so none
could read it. I was asked to get
your name by several men agreeing
you were certainly the game
to play, until I told them who
you were. I prize the look that they
accorded me, a connoisseur of
beauty, you, a life's reward.

Morning Glory

It is a comely flower
even though it's common.
I like it, and I'm glad it chose
to grow beside the balcony
along the curious wire going to the roof
where our apartment joins the next.

No one else can see it,
secret flower greeting me from semi-shadow,
shy to everyone but opening to me.

Beside me you begin to stretch,
the balcony ignored,
transformed from sleep
into my morning glory.

Necklace

Because I cannot go with you
and hang around you all day long,
to see you clip and snip,
tease and spike,
shampoo and perm
a dozen heads
before we meet for lunch,
I may just imagine what it's like
to be there with you.

Instead, I'll send my spy,
the emerald necklace
that I gave to you last Christmas,
pretend the green eye is a camera,
seeing you interact so freely
with whomever occupies your chair
and feels your fingers in their hair,
and hang suspended all day
blissfully in motion
between your breasts.

Hands

My own hand on the gear shift
scraped at one knuckle
from a rough engine mount,
small hairs covering the backside
and between the joints
up to the pink skin
under milky nails,
dirt-ended.

Silent.

Waiting for the soft skin
of your hand
to fold over it,
tiny wrinkles where each finger
spreads to match my own.

Post-Fireworks

Two weeks before our wedding
we went to the fireworks
at the park.
The day was hot and you
wore a thin coral-colored halter
that had every adolescent
male in awe.
After hot dogs and lemonade
we settled in the drip zone
of a willow
and waited for the dark.

Today we have no tree,
just folding chairs
on the balcony,
and dark is almost here.

The fireworks we saw
bursting in the July sky
are gone,
but tonight,
the clouds all
hump and point like hearts
to celebrate
our private
interdependence.

Sunburn

The thing
about these last few
summer days is that I
never think the sun is quite so hot
and I forget to put some sunscreen on.
Now at night, with the cicadas laughing,
you must pay the price with me,
by rubbing aloe all across my
shoulders, giving pleasure
to me even in
my pain.

Car Wash

Vinegar and water
is the best solution for
the mess that some offending dog
has left in marking territory
on your right rear whitewall.

And if I have to clean that up,
I may as well wash off the rest
as well, to make it shine
the way your smile shines for me.

It's little in return
for all the coruscating strokes
you've shown the chassis of my life.

Bee Sting

You had chosen to slip off your
sandals and carry them
as we walked through
the clover and buttercups
down by the stream
at the park.

The happy birdsong
and playful breeze
took our attention
from the unpleasant
realities of life.

You killed a bee,
unseen,
who stung between your toes
with its dying reflex.

Under the yellow maple
throbbing red,
you rubbed and cried,
and I had nothing
to relieve your pain
and could not kiss away
the tears that formed.

I could only murmur,
"I'm sorry,"
and with each repetition
contract a little more inside
from knowing
I had failed.

Folding Laundry While You Are Away

Warm and not quite dry, each sock, each
random piece of underwear, each
towel, a reminder of your
presence in each day. Each cotton
fabric tells me you have substance
giving shape to flaccid cloth and
also to my life. The ankle-
length short socks have swelled with toes and
tarsals, just as I have grown more
fulsome since you came into my
world. Your panties, simple, soft, and
supple, match the flesh that weekly
fills them, touch your buttocks and in
doing so define their shape, and
in this way suggest the cleft that
marks the two-part structure of your
place in marriage, lover, worker,
both in equal parts. Your bra: still
clinging to the things around it,
lucky cloth that rubs your breasts, your
nipples with each turn and stretch you
make throughout your day—my lips, my
palms, my fingers volunteer to
take your place on any day you
need a rest—and let your breasts give
loving shape to me. The towel,
luckiest of all, not only
sees you naked every day but
touches, rubs, caresses every
part of you, a service I am
glad to carry on instead as
often as you want to ask me.

Soft Scent

Lavender, melon,
a hint of ginger—
even in sleep
your soft scent whispers
infrared aroma
on unseen wavelengths,
clean and pure,
alive and warm,
not forbidden but undisturbed—
your sleep is precious.

I am content to take you in
with each breath,
lungs contracting and releasing
your essence,
joining us in
soft
olfactory
embraces.

Hole Nine

The dogleg on the eighth hole always beats me,
and I end up in the trees.
I've lost more balls there
than on all the other holes combined.
The trampling in the brush
beneath the oaks and cedars
always feels like failure,
wasted time,
the way my life was
in the days before we met.

Today I got a hole in one from hole nine—
that must have been the honeymoon,
the miracle that turned ill fortune upside down.

I Took Three Books

I took three books from your shelf
to see if I could learn more
about the way you think,
but you will always be a mystery to me.

I looked in Yeats' *Collected Poems*
and found a fairy world that
turned to disillusionment
to incomprehensibility.

I looked at *Sense and Sensibility*
but never made it past
the hard-heart sister-in-law
and petty dreams of Marianne.

My final try was Shakespeare,
where I understood more words than I expected,
but it's not the kind of thing that
I can pick up on my own.

I decided I would stick with football
as a way to stimulate my mind.

Balcony Flower

I don't know what that flower is you've grown out on the balcony
in seven feet of sun, but you've done it well,
because the delicate pink blossoms—
more than pink,
I have no word for
that new wavelength's tint—
remind me that the tender care
you show for it is small
compared to what you
show for me—
what can I call that?—
some emotion,
dedication,
wondrous flower
I can't put a name on.

Buying Sanitary Napkins

"Richard, I need something from the store," you say
as I walk past the bathroom door. "Sure, Sweets. What is it?"
Then the pause that should have waved a red flag at me,
but it didn't. I turn back to hear you better,
in the doorway sense your insecurity—
or is it mine? You hold the empty package up
for me to see. "No, anything but—" then I hear,
"for better or for worse," and force a smile, nod,
and snatch the keys from off the hook. I'm sure that men
buy things like that—I tell myself while looking in
the rearview mirror—every day. But I am not
convinced. I've never seen it done. Then in the aisle
panic strikes—so many choices—which one matches
anything I can recall? In resolution
I scoop up the nearest one, and gaining
confidence I ask, what shame, embarrassment is there
in doing what you need? I pick the shortest line and
hand my purchase to the clerk. I look her in
the eye and say, "I would do anything for her."
She shrugs and rings me up, unmoved, but I have fought
the dragon and will do so every time you ask.

I Smell Onions

I smell onions on your breath and
think of Shakespeare's wire-haired mistress.
You, too, submit to gravity
                                and time.
There's no mistaking
your pretty human voice
for birdsong,
no wings or halo to confuse
my dull mortal senses.

For all the beauty of the nightingale's call
and the sudden thrill of heavenly annunciation,
I'd rather hear you,
                stepping through the doorway,
                                        say my name,
with plain old
fallible
human
affection.

Sick Day

You woke feverish and achy,
and you knew you couldn't meet
the obligations of the day.
You said you wanted me to shoot you,
but I knew you meant
your head was throbbing
and your back hurt.

After giving you some tea and pills,
I told you, "Close your eyes and just relax."
Though I was dressed
and ready to do other things,
I lay myself beside you
and began to rub your shoulders,
firm caresses that as much said that I cared
as it addressed the tensions.
One hand moving gently, surely
on your back,
the other making airy circles
in your hair,
those were the words you needed.

And when you began to snore,
I took some satisfaction that I'd made
a difference that no medicine could make.

I left you sleeping, hoping
that the next time that you woke,
if I were gone,
you'd still remember
my ten fingers
on you
speaking love.

Watching You Sleep

Your cheek is smooth, relaxed,
your shoulder slowly rising, ebbing
where the blanket stops.
The doctor says you need your rest,
more rest than usual—
you're young and strong,
but things have gotten in your body,
things that don't belong there,
making *young* and *strong*
seem distant and unreal.

But even in your sickness,
I can see
the edges of your mouth—
well, one side—
curving upward, just a bit,
as if the place where you are now
is much more pleasant
than the ailing frame
that holds you in reality.

I see you've left your shirt off,
from your temperature, perhaps,
but in my heart I hope that it's for me,
that even in your disconnectedness,
you thought that I would come to check on you,
and maybe see your skin that I so much admire,
just a peek,
a glimpse of
your affection for me,
even ill.
And that must be the thing
that makes you smile
knowing even in your sleep
that I am watching over you.

Making Progress

You are ashamed
at having been in bed so long, you say,
but sickness isn't something to feel shame for.
Bodies do what bodies do.
You dream of being well again,
of hiking and of shopping (not online)
and doing simple things like cutting hair.
But you can't stand the whole day long yet—
Pat will take your place at work
another day or two.

So when you ask me to stay home
instead of heading out to golf,
I make a call and drop my bag,
and lie beside you,
hold your hand,
and snuggle while we watch
The Mexican, your favorite movie,
for the seventh time.
When Winston Baldry tells Samantha
real love never says "enough,"
my eyes tear up,
and I know you are not
the only one who's getting better.

Visit

I don't mind
your mother visiting—
it gives me time
to show her
      that I love you
        in so many ways
        she's never seen before,
      a level of consideration
        she has not suspected
        since she turned her heart from men.
And I can
      learn to understand her better, too,
      dissolve some bitterness, perhaps,
        associated with my gender,
      treat her well because
        she is the one who gave you life,
          the one who makes my happiness exist.

Old Photograph

At first I thought the photograph was yours,
an old-time souvenir from some amusement kiosk,
till I saw the pick-up in the distance
and I knew it was an heirloom
from another generation. But the likeness
is uncanny, and I wonder
what temptations she endured
before she made the choice that led her
to conceive your mother. In those days,
did she have several suitors every weekend
men who saw her face
and volunteered to give their time,
their strength, affection, lives
to live in sight of her each day,
as I have done to be in sight of you?

Your Mother's Scar

You told me of the scar that marked
your birth today: across your mother's
abdomen, a bigger slash than I'd imagined,
one that could not be ignored.
I wonder if she sees it when she dresses
and remembers that she would have lost you
had it not been for the scalpel,
lost you as she did the child
some years later when its heart stopped beating
in the womb. The scar is yours—the painful
advent, painful memory she treasures.
She must carry other scars as well,
the scar of absent husband and the scar
of isolation when you said you had to
go to college out of state. And I am
certainly no doctor like she prayed
that you would marry. But she visits with a
smile, keeps the scars concealed because
to wish the scars away would be to lose
the pleasure that you brought as well, the pride
of county beauty queen, the satisfaction
that you mattered to the world for that
bright moment. More than that she holds your friendship
as the dearest thing in life. I know
she would not trade your scar for anything.

The Stars Last Night

More stars were born last night,
since the storm had scrubbed the air
and a power line was down somewhere.
We sat in the dark for an hour,
just soaking starbeams on the balcony,
enjoying the touch of each other's hand.
You said you thought the stars above the bank
looked something like a stadium,
with athletes all in place for some sharp competition.
You kissed my hand when I said
the stadium was really just a heart
with a thousand points of love shining just for us.
Then after several moments,
I heard you moving,
and the rustling of your clothes.
You reached my buttons,
stood me up,
and we stood naked underneath the stars,
your arms around me tight.
"Not a stadium,
not a heart,"
you said,
"It's me."
And you straddled me across the chair
and asked me to keep
making constellations in you
as long as I desired.

Fretting

You are more than thirty minutes late
and I wonder if I should have checked
the oil before you left this morning ...
or the tires ...
or the battery.

And why has your cell phone message
gone generic?
Should I go to look for you ...
or wait a while longer for the sheriff's call
to say they've found your car ...
your purse ...
your corpse?

I feel the panic of the thought of life without you,
a hole without a doughnut
growing to the space between the stars
and just as vacuous.

When I hear the car
and reach the door to see you,
the emptiness contracts again
to fit into your smile
and is swallowed up
just as the pizza in your arms
will be.

Tuesday Morning Thanks

I guess it might seem silly,
but I wanted you to know,
last night
while we did many lovely things together,
one expressed your love for me superbly—
when you sat across my lap
and put one arm
across my shoulders,
saying nothing,
satisfied to occupy
the very place I was
until the game was over,
holding me content.

Weekend

i. Hiking

Your legs seem longer
with those short socks and gym shorts.
I can't help but notice, following you
up the hiking trail along the creek.
The gurgle and birdchirp chorus replace
the car horn and tire whizz of the work week,
letting tension relax,
even as the muscles work
double-time.

The poise of a long-forsaken ballet stretch
is still in you as we cross the creek,
reaching, hopping, straining to stay
on the providential rocks,
knowing wet shoes do not hike well,
and when I fall against you,
and you hold me with both arms and body,
your legs push us back in kilter.

On the other side, the trail, much broader,
lets us tread abreast,
my stride measuring to yours,
step by step,
socially
emotionally
tactilely
purposefully
together.

ii. Picnic

None of the other hikers
have come this far today,
and we stop to eat
beside a pond
among the trees.

We are not the first to see it—
the trail nearby attests to that—
but we are here alone.

You have set
your shoes and socks
beside us
and put your feet
into the water
while we wonder
at a world inverted,
sky so deep
beneath the double-pointed pines.

We eat our bread and drink our wine,
communing in a dim unspoken memory,
like a couple, oh, so long ago.

Stan Galloway

iii. Campfire

Distant geese call goodnight
to us and one another
from the pond.
The foil that blackened around our potatoes
breaks the low light in a hundred ways,
unnatural mirror, strange and lifeless.
The trees and rocks around us
melt together
into nothing,
leaving just us two
alone in lighted limbo.

In the charcoal glow, your hair is red and gold,
like Christmas wrap ahead of season,
your skin alight,
commanding my attention.
The shimmer circling your face betokens
more than mortal grace,
and I wonder if the pantheon
is short one goddess.

Just Married

iv. Morning

I can hear the other campers stirring—
clanks and claps ride on the breeze outside.
A butter yellow glow suffuses us inside the tent.
Your back to me, exposed and innocent, reminds me
while we said we wanted to make love
we fell asleep before the foreplay ended.
Now stiff and disappointed
that the holiday is coming to a close,
I have to shift my thinking
to remember the delight we've had together,
memories we've made,
in love.
There's nothing wrong,
I tell myself,
in tiredness,
especially from activity together.
We'll pack the tent and travel home.
Tonight we'll be untired and
we'll rub the stiffness out.

Reverie

After your shower,
I see you from the doorway
sitting at the bed edge,
towel puddled at your feet.

You are motionless,
one foot pulled up beside you,
where you had been looking at your toenails,
one arm out the other way for balance,
a kind of sculpted Galatea
rising from a marble bed,
enfleshed,
        alive,
           absorbed.

Your toes are now forgotten
as you look wide at nothing,
        at a space outside the room
              inside yourself,
captured by the muse
       a memory,
       a random coupling of incongruous thoughts.

I wonder if you think of me
but dare not enter,
knowing how a bubble,
         poem,
           or thought
can burst to soapfilm
at the slightest prick.

Later when I ask,
you say you don't remember.

Morning Hair

I have to laugh   when your hair sticks out
in angles formed   by the pillow folds
the morning after   dinner out.
I know you spent,   the night before,
a pleasant remembrance,   painstaking hours
getting every   glamorous sweep
to fall just so,   as females back
before the pen   prepared themselves
for special nights   with special men.
I wonder now,   this waking moment,
if vanity   or vain conceit was
deep down at the root.   Or did desire,
warm or hot,   hunger or whim,
prod a woman's   preparations?
Did she feel less   a woman, laughter
greeting her   in morning hair,
or laugh along   in light assent,
assured her place,   fixed and proper,
unlike her hair,   in lover's heart?

Hair Drying

When I saw you
just out of the shower
both arms raised,
towel mulched around your ankles,
hair blowing from the dryer you so deftly shook—
in that soft domestic image
hair became a crown of leaves
and naked flesh became,
like Daphne's,
blotted bark,
the Chinese elm that
grew outside my bedroom.

It was the tree where
I first learned to climb
to shinny
trust my arms to hold my weight
when my short legs would shift,
to stretch and seat in untried ways
to gain an inch or two.
I learned to trust my body in that tree
and when I'd reached a dizzying height
two body lengths above the ground,
I'd grab a branch and pendulum around like Tarzan
landing with a satisfying feet-first smack against the earth
my arms stretched wide in seven-year-old pride,
my own Olympic champion.

Just Married

You set the blower down
and pull the plug—
you turn
and see me watching, smiling,
never knowing how the sight of you
touches both the man and boy
that live inside of me.

Three-Month Anniversary

I'll take you out tonight
for Japanese cuisine
and hope that it surprises
and delights you that
I noticed we've been married
three months now, a lifetime
yet so little. Our first
date you wanted to eat
sushi, something I had
never tried before,
but I was willing, always
have been game, with you,
for something new. I liked it—
something decadent
and bold about it that said,
"This is real life, not that
dull impostor you've been
tasting all along,"
or was it you that made me
feel that way?

Delight

The thing that constantly amazes me
about you is how little things delight,
like holding hands or watching stars. You'd think
the pink carnation that I brought you with the
groceries was a precious heirloom and the
spring roll with our supper was expensive
caviar from Finland. You're so good
at showing your appreciation in your
smile and your eyes that anything
beyond becomes extravagant and makes
me richer than a common man should be.

Making Love the One Hundredth Time

I keep remembering the words you said last night.

While you were in the bathroom, I brought in a hundred
red balloons, so many you could hardly take
a step. You laughed and threw the nearest one at me,
where I lay propped, expectant, at the pillow end
of our firm double bed. I laughed when you, so naked,
just like me, scared up a flock of red balloons
to sudden flight, before you settled, face to face,
our sexes just a practiced space apart. You asked
what was the reason, and I smugly said this marked
the hundredth time that you and I made love together.

Open-mouthed, surprisingly perplexed, you thought
before you answered diplomatically that you
supposed a different number. When you asked me just
how long ago I thought it was we last made love,
I thought that you were joking. Clearly it had been
the night before. What was it, then, you asked, this morning
at the breakfast table when you cupped my breast
and kissed me deep and long—was there no love made then?
And after work, when our hands touched and our eyes locked
a hundred times while cleaning up the dishes—that was
making love, you said; how cheated I must be
to not know making love goes on throughout the day
and isn't boxed into a single naked act.

Missing You

The night you stayed with Rachel when she lost her child
was the first we'd been apart. You cut and styled
several women's hair to keep her mind distracted
from the dream deflated, knowing how impacted
long before your mother was. I missed you—you
with all your girlfriends giving mercy, comfort, beauty,
in a time of loss. My loss was small compared
to hers, but no less real. It was because you cared
about someone beyond yourself, a virtue I
need practice on, that I was forced to sleep—and cry—
alone. I can't resent your mercy, but the knowledge
did not take away the emptiness. The hallway,
kitchen, bedroom, echoed with your absence, heatless,
till we came together the next day—so sweet.

Hat

You dressed as Dorothy Parker for the party,
some dead woman I have never heard of,
as if anyone would know her by her dress.
You say the hat's what makes it obvious.
Now Crocodile Dundee has a hat
that's known the world around—
or maybe Indiana Jones' fedora
snags some recognition,
but Dorothy Parker's hat, I fear,
is only what you call it—
no one else will know or care—
they'll humor you perhaps,
pretend they know,
but really as a costume
you have chosen something too obscure.
But when I say you must get out more,
smiling, you touch my chest
and dent the S for Superman
and tell me, "Au contraire,
it's you who needs to read more."

Tire-Changing

Except the time lost, I don't mind a tire change.
The unexpected doesn't ruffle me too much.
But last night was a mess: the wind and rain beside
the road, and, urging me to hurry, your voice splintered
by the window lowered just a fingertip
and rain-bolts rattling against my head and filling
up the hubcap. Spray from passing drivers added
road grit to my hair and clothes and flashlight lens.
Those thirteen minutes felt like thirteen hours and
it seemed the natural world was all against me, 'til
I sogged back to the car, the spare in place, and you
said, "Nothing but a hot bath when we're home," and I
knew even Nature couldn't thwart a woman's love.

Celebrate

You cried
when Mary Jane stood at the door
of Peter Parker's room
prepared to take the risk of loving,
even when it meant the loss
of her security.

I didn't understand
how much you gave up
when you said you'd marry me.
My job can pay the rent
and basic needs
but little else,
and no one knows my name
the way your mother's name is known.
(And on the sly,
I don't surf city streets on webs
to right the wrongs of millions.)

But if the truth be known,
I wish that I could wrap you up
and save your life.

We'll celebrate
each ordinary day we share.

Next Best

Frozen peas bounce
       fourteen new directions
              on the kitchen floor.
The cutting board of peppers
       and the lettuce in the bowl
              will be less balanced now without them,
but the salad will still work,
       and if I get them swept up quickly
              you may never know the change
       between the thing I had intended
and the thing I offered you.

How often do I give you
less than what I wanted—
did you forfeit anything,
never having the original—
and is a present measured
by its coining thought?

I don't want to hide things,
       even small
              from you,
so I leave
       the swept-up peas
              at the top of the trash,
offering my lesser best this time,
       but planning that my next best
              will be better.

Scraping the Windshield

The first of Autumn's frosts
has crept across our windshields
while we slept.

I start my pickup then I turn to your car,
take my visa card, and
scrape the frozen, sight-obscuring film,
so you can go
without the unexpected need
to clear the window.

You may never notice,
since the sun might do the same,
but I'll do it anyway.

Watching You Read in Bed

What do you read there, for I want to know—
that yellow book of ancient deeds and quaint
philosophy? Is it embarrassed looking
back at chest exposed, or does it care
that public text is privately obsessed?
And why am I perplexed that you enjoy
the reading when I am detained by joyless
tasks? Can I be jealous or refrain
from noticing? What can I tell, except
I wish I were the one who wrote the words
that enter you like fish into the streams
where they will spawn; I wish I were the tent
that lies along your bent and naked legs;
I wish I were the book that begs your full
attention any daytime pause, that looks
a foot away at nipples, succulent,
and tipping siren swells of tactile gold,
that feels your hands that hold me firmly in
your pliant lap and steals my body, object
of your pleasure, at your timely will.

Apology

Give me back the words I spoke
that stung you like a hailstone
in the rain. I don't know
where they came from,
what imp urged
the battle in my tongue,
some malevolent,
invisible,
unwanted spirit.

Give them back so I can grind them
into powder and dispose of them
in one grand flush
or mad triumphant flash of fireworks,
this time for good.

Give them back
because they did not
represent my heart—
a heated tongue
extended from a neutral brain,
a moaning of insensible wind
in a Rocky Mountain storm,
destructive,
meaning nothing.

Give me back the words—
oh—if you could only
give me back the words.

Shopping

I stopped to look at cereal
and didn't notice you'd moved on
until you'd nearly reached the aisle end.
When I looked up and saw you,
my heart jumped
in mixed delight and consternation.
You, the woman branded in my brain and heart
were reaching to a shelf,
contorting in a foreign way
but with the same straight waist
and rounded hips I know so well,
the strain of cotton leaving little to imagine,
in one hand a paper and a pen
and in the other what I couldn't recognize,
just as the light and store-shelf frame caused me
to wonder at the profile of your face
and from such distance question,
can it be the
soft-lipped,
clear-skinned,
ginger-scented
woman that is you?

Watching Football

I didn't mean to tune your voice out
when you asked for my attention,
but the Redskins tied the Cowboys
with a minute left to play.
I treated you as if the game were
more important, as if I could
have your voice, your care, your love,
on my time, when the truth is, you should
be the center of my thoughts and
hearing you be paramount,
and I forget, and need to ask you
once again for your forgiveness
(and point out that I could hear you
so much better when the Redskins
won the game in overtime).

Pie Making

I rubbed your feet until you fell asleep.
It's not too late, so I will fix a pie
for you, no special reason. Pumpkin is your
favorite so I get a can that I'd been
saving at the back of one high shelf
and check below for some evaporated
milk. Two cans, two eggs, two people, mixed
together with some cinnamon and nutmeg
and a dash of cloves and ginger that
bring out the flavors of each day. A couple
shakes of salt to mark the tears that sometimes
fall to make the sugar all the sweeter.
Then I pull a pie crust from the freezer
where I'd stacked and stored a dozen some weeks
earlier in preparation for the
holidays, and slip it in the oven
for an hour, while I think of how
you've entered in this doughy, crusty life
of mine and made it one delicious treat.

Seeing Straight

You gave me just a glimpse tonight
of what you have inside.
You cried while we were watching *Ratatouille*,
odd because it seems irrelevant
to what you said. I thank you for your efforts
to explain that an insensitive
old man had said you couldn't see straight
when you cut his hair today
and that you couldn't shake the words
your father said, "Some day you'll see straight, darling,
and agree my leaving's for the best."
You haven't understood for fifteen years,
you said, and now you feel you never will,
that seeing straight will always be
beyond your grasp. And though I said
some people's straight is pretty crooked
and I held you while you cried,
I realized not even you and I
will always find agreement,
but that doesn't mean
we have to leave
each other's arms.

Giving Space

I guess it's only natural when you say
you want some space. The thing that's riding you,
you say, is something that you've got to deal with
on your own. It's not dishonesty
because you've told me right up front, but it's
a secret and it feels like a betrayal.
Why you won't confide in me perplexes
and confounds me since I've given you
a lifetime as companion and a promise
to walk through it all with you. I honor
your request with a reminder that
when you come out the other side,
I'm waiting here for you.

Milk Jug

I took an empty milk jug from the fridge
and knew it had been you who put it there,
but why?

a joke to make me eat my corn flakes dry?
or was it spite because I didn't wash the car when you had asked?
a phone call as you cleared your things by habit?

Was I on your mind,
or was the jug as full of milk
as you were full of me?

Storm Thoughts

The storm is moving fast
across a three-state swath
and I'm sure to be at best
in some hotel
instead of home with you,
that is, if I can find a vacancy.
The radio announced
the interstate is closed now,
and I've got nothing I can do
but lick my wounds.
But I remember what you said,
that though our bodies might be far apart,
together is state of mind.

That's when I dream
through snow drifts in the street
that I'm cozy
by the fireplace
with you.
We are touching hands together,
tapping cups together,
feeling heat together,
in my favorite winter dream.

Car Show

You weren't exactly thrilled when I
invited you to drive an hour with me
to the car show. But you came with me
as usual because the time we spend together,
even bored, is better than the prospect of
a half a day apart. And in the end,
you seemed to like the fondness
that I felt for older makes,
especially the dark blue Ford from '56,
a pickup with a narrow box.

It gave you comfort, I could tell, that,
when the new and sleeker models come along,
my interests won't be charmed
to losing love of classic ordinary frames
grown old along with me.

Weighing In

You complain you've gotten fat—your clothes
no longer fit the way they did because
your thighs are thicker, buttocks rounder, tummy
pushing at the snaps. It doesn't comfort
you for me to say I didn't notice—
neither would it help to say I did.
You surely know that you are not
your body shape—size 3 or size 16
will do the job of holding in
the thing that's you, the essence deep
inside the skin. But knowing that
does little to relieve the doubt
your weight has made on your self-worth,
so take my hand and let's go walking
to the park where we can jump
and swing and revel in the shapes
and frames of mind
we used to be.

Some Kinds of Love

When we babysat my nephew
and you held him cradled in your arms,
though he was far from newborn,
I was thinking of a child of our own,
composed of you and me in equal parts,
and knew that was a kind of love
I did not know.

And when he spit the food out,
wet the chair,
and bit my nose,
I realized
some kinds of love
are more persistence
than delight,
some kinds of love
might benefit
from waiting for a while.

Nursing the Kitten

It was found in a shopping bag left at the cart
return mewing so faintly I would have passed on
had you not checked my arm. When you cuddled it later
that night in your lap with a medicine dropper
for surrogate teat, it confusedly stirred,
still abandoned at heart, and its eyes, still untested
yet following whisker-felt warmth, looked in vain
for a something that can't be defined, intuition-
guessed only. Still later you set it, not asking,
between us in bed, something foreignly soft,
softly foreign. It nuzzled the dropper as I
nuzzle you, using nose, using lips all aquiver
in anticipation of milkless affection.
The next day the shelter accepted our orphan
but we are left shadowed, and I am nonplussed.

Stan Galloway

The Ring

the ring upon your finger
circles back to where it started,
always moving on and reaching back—
a symbol of the single art that lacks a name
(called love sometimes, or sin, or heart, a practiced game
for some): the constant and embodied fact
that every turn that tugs apart
is cause to re-begin

108

Long Lunch

I'm sitting at the empty picnic table in the park,
the one beside the river where you said you'd meet me,
wondering what's taking you so long.

If the lateness is involuntary, did your car refuse to start,
or did a patron keep you working,
talking far beyond the time you break for lunch?
Did you take ill or lose your phone to call me?

Though this is a standard hour,
it is the longest lunch I've had since meeting you
since lunches are too short when we're together.

Remembering Waikiki

Unnumbered days have passed
since we looked out on Waikiki,
but I remember still the ocean, vast
as love itself. The first night's moon slow-burned,
by raw decree, in salty urn
of Cupid's potpourri.

Out on the balcony,
in ruffling wind, we both discerned
the steady waves, assumed a guarantee
our bliss—as sure—would certainly outlast
the airy turn of moonlight cast
on water-driven churn.

Beguiled, I did not learn
each clap of sand and wave recast
the grain and substance of each small concern
to subtly alter facets by degree.
What does not last becomes debris.
Each *now* becomes the past.

Headache

Oh.
You say you have a headache.
I believe you.
But the way you said it
makes me wonder
if the headache is from me,
that my attentions make you hurt,
because you want less.
I have never tried to take
what is not offered.
Have I thought, though,
some things offered
that were given grudgingly,
in duty not in joy?
Your love of subtle metaphors
(like those you read in books)
and indirection
makes me wonder.
I don't know what lies
behind those eyelids now.
Did I misunderstand?
Perhaps you mumbled *heartache*.

Cleaning the Tub

Soap scum is a mystery to me—
how does something
that's supposed to clean
require cleaning of itself?
Soap and water take
the dirt and sloughed-off skin cells
from our bodies well enough,
then why does it accumulate
on tub and shower walls?

To have to clean
the thing that cleans us
just seems wrong—
like chewing up
the same bite twice.

The only motivation that I have
is knowing you won't
get into a tub
with me
that's dirty,
and it's that perspective
that gives purpose to the
scrubbing,
scraping,
wiping,
rinsing.
work
before me now.

Sable Dress

I'd never seen that dress before,
so elegant,
a backless, sleeveless sable silk
that clung—but didn't,
shifting shape so subtly
as to make mirages real
and deft deception
all at once.

I smiled every minute of the office party,
knowing you were there with me,
and knowing all the others knew it too.

The only prick in my balloon
was when you said you'd worn it
to your senior prom,
with someone now whose name escapes you,
someone who had felt
that silk upon you long before.

Rust

A strip of bubbles underneath
the paint beneath the driver's door
foretells a problem (that is, if I
don't address it soon), from last year's
winter weather. Oxidation
is the enemy of every
metal part, unnoticed, eating
at the very molecules,
bringing instability,
destroying what was made. I've got to
grind away the paint and what's
beneath, down to the metal, smooth it,
treat it, paint it.
          Now if only
fixing brokenness between us
were so easy.

Makeup

I'd never noticed the care before
you use when putting on
your makeup—
many layers, subtle,
to achieve the perfect look.

You hide the darker lines
beneath your eyes,
then darken lids above;
you highlight brows and lashes
to bring definition, contrast.

The slight blush
that I thought I brought to you
comes really from a
dab and rub of several sponges,
and the tingle when we kiss,
I should have known,
is one of three slick layers,
artificially applied.

Mapping Spilled Milk

Door slap—
engine rev—
you're gone
to work—
both of us
stung by
parting
words

I look to where the milk has spilled across the table,
two separate shapes: the smaller one Vermont, I think,
                    the other nearer me is Florida—
                    one small and maple sweet,
                    one long and gritty.
                    Before I leave
                    I push the two together
                    with the dishcloth,
                    soaking up the bulk
                    but leaving
                    some swampland,
                    treacherous ground we're on,
                    hoping things will
                    dry while we're apart
                    and I can return
                    New Hampshire
                    to you.

Cooking Pasta

I set dishes at the table,
not speaking to your back at the stove.
Water's boiling.
You spill spaghetti from the box, long and firm,
more fragile than thought.
It distorts
  and
    grows soft.

Just Married 2

I thought marriage meant
    you would touch me every day
    you would delight in me
    you would understand there were two sides
                    to every coin,

but I see marriage means
    touching may not happen
    delight has many objects
    understanding does not mean sympathy.

When touching goes,
        delight diffuses,
              and understanding fails to join us,
I am just married.

Winter Weather

When your love for me is like
a woodchuck in November,
cold,
unmoving,
barely breathing,
and the forecast is for
sleet and snow,
I pull my pores in tighter
underneath the anorak
I've struggled into.

Yet, if this November
last a thousand days,
I will remain to start December,
never backing out
toward September's sun
but moving for
the always-sought-for April.

About the Author

 **Stan Galloway** teaches writing and literature at Bridgewater College, in the heart of Virginia's Shenandoah Valley. His work has appeared in print and online in places such as *Boston Literary Magazine, Connotation Press, Contemporary World Literature, Flutter Poetry Journal, Hobo Camp Review, Loch Raven Review, The Muse: An International Journal of Poetry, Paradise Review, Red Booth Review, Scarlet Literary Magazine,* and *vox poetica*. His work has been nominated Best of the Net by three different editors. *Just Married* is his first full-length collection of poems. He has written a chapbook, *Abraham* (Sierra Delta Press, 2012) and a book of literary analysis, *The Teenage Tarzan* (McFarland, 2010).

Publication Credits

Grateful acknowledgment is made to the following where some of the poems (or earlier versions) first appeared:

Alligator Stew: Unpacking the Suitcase
A Bird's Life (Books on Blog): The Art of Introduction (3rd place in the 2012 Elizabeth Neuwirth Memorial contest sponsored by The Poetry Society of Virginia), Feeding Ducks
Boston Literary Magazine: Makeup, Walking on the Beach
Camel Saloon: Rust
Eunoia Review: Just Married, Milk Jug
In Motion Magazine: Honolulu Elevator, Morning Coffee
Loch Raven Review: Folding Laundry While You Are Away
Muddy River Poetry Review: Car Show
Seek It: Writers and Artists Do Sleep (Red Claw Press): Morning Hair, Watching You Read in Bed
vox poetica: Apology, Hat, I Smell Onions (1st place in vox poetica's First Ever Poetry Contest), The Piano Promise, Post-Fireworks, Remembering Waikiki, Reverie, Sable Dress

Special thanks go to Bridgewater College for sabbatical leave during which a portion of this book was completed.

Praise for *Just Married*

Stan Galloway has created a world of classic love, and the trials of maintaining that love, into a realm all its own. When I read his poetry I see the impenetrable depths of affection often seen in Pablo Neruda wed to a slightly smirky reality of Charles Bukowski. Throughout *Just Married* there is a narrative thread that keeps to a single story, yet, at any point the reader can randomly open to a page and gain the prize of a whole novel unto itself. Galloway utilizes speech of the common man while sneaking in deep-rooted connections to cosmology and mythology that add a timeless, classical tone to his text. Love is not always glorious. It is not always new and ethereal with the smell of roses and fresh sex. Yet, Galloway says that's okay, more than okay, and if it falls apart, the gods won't hate us for it. For any hopeless romantic who's no stranger to dips in the road, *Just Married* is a map from the heights of amore to the depth of barroom blues where we try to figure out where it all went wrong—then raise a glass to making it right the next go-around.

—Clifford Brooks
Author of *The Draw of Broken Eyes & Whirling Metaphysics*

"Just Married" reads the trailing kite
Someone has rigged to hover aft.

But promptly at the second light
It breaks its tether—just like us.

Stan Galloway's *Just Married* follows the undercurrents of love, from earliest infatuation through to devotion, tattered and scarred, but still holding on, holding out. These poems carefully track the minutiae that go into the building of a life together: the words, the fights, the quality of light on a beloved face. Galloway doesn't promise a fantasy, but instead something infinitely more lasting: to make each day extraordinary nonetheless. These are poems offered wholeheartedly, ultimately blindsided by the heart's other propensity—to change.

—Jenna Butler
Faculty, Grant McEwan University
Author of *Aphelion* and *Wells*

In *Just Married*, the observations of Stan Galloway's mildly perturbed speaker, a groom innocently romantic and in naive awe of what's to come, invites us along as he moves from rehearsal to church to honeymoon, even into the bedroom, sharing each small but crucial epiphany as he encounters the realities of a life so shared. In "Unpacking the Suitcase," his nude bride chooses clothing from her opened suitcase while the groom discovers that "there were many/other things you'd packed, things unexpected—" As the unexpected continues to be revealed—that his own nipples are as sensitive as those of his wife, that her bra makes a serviceable tourniquet, that a marriage's foundation tends to settle in less than ideal ways—our husband comes to see that "marriage means/touching may not happen/delight has many objects/ understanding does not mean sympathy."

—John Hoppenthaler,
Associate Professor of English/Creative Writing
East Carolina University

Just Married is not just a romantic assembly of poems with snippets of real, plausible scenarios between a newly married couple, it is an actual insight into Galloway's heart placed eloquently on the page. The poet's true talent has always been his ability to be sentimental without being too fluffy, and humorous without being too silly. He again achieves these things in this collection with his unique and balanced narrative style. It is a must read for all poetry lovers and the perfect gift for the newly married couple.

—Julie Ellinger Hunt
Pushcart Prize nominated poet
Author of *Ever Changing* and *In New Jersey*

Other Titles Published by unbound CONTENT

A Bank Robber's Bad Luck With His Ex-Girlfriend
By KJ Hannah Greenberg

A Strange Frenzy
By Dom Gabrielli

At Age Twenty
By Maxwell Baumbach

Before the Great Troubling
By Corey Mesler

Captured Moments
By Ellenelizabeth Cernek

Elegy
By Raphaela Willington

Garden
By Ellen Kline McLeod

In New Jersey
By Julie Ellinger Hunt

Inspiration 2 Smile
By Nate Spears

Painting Czeslawa Kwoka: Honoring Children of the Holocaust
By Theresa Senato Edwards and Lori Schreiner

Saltian
By Alice Shapiro

The Pomegranate Papers
This is how honey runs
By Cassie Premo Steele

Written All Over Your Face{book}
By PMPope

18837688R00070

Made in the USA
Charleston, SC
23 April 2013